IN THE BEGINNING

There was no thing
in the beginning

No thing to see feel hear or read
Now there is this book
Written by a human
That was not in the beginning

WOW

The Present is Sacred

Danny Brantley

Published by Danny Brantley, 2024.

THE PRESENT IS SACRED

First edition. April 12, 2024.

Copyright © 2024 Danny Brantley.

ISBN: 979-8224986699

Written by Danny Brantley.

Table of Contents

JESUS AND THOSE I LOVE 1
JESUS KNEW 2
BUMPER STICKER...3
A PLACE I LOVE 4
BIRTHDAY OF THE SONG 5
HAIL OF FORTY POUNDS 6
A MESSAGE FROM JESUS 7
JUST BECAUSE...8
EARTH HUMAN LIFETIME 9
JESUS IS..10
A TOAST FOR RED WINE 11
GOD'S LOVE...12
IRREPARABLE 13
COVID TIME 14
LOVE AND FRIENDSHIP 16
LIFE..17
A TEAR...18
DOMAIN..19
IF YOU LOVE 20
WE LEARN 21
ELECTION 2020 USA 22
INAUGURATION DAY 2021 23
FREEDOM 25
GOOD DOCTORS 2020 26
GHASTLY TORMENT 27
A MAN ON HIS HORSE 28
GOD'S BEAUTIFUL VISION..29
HOLY SPIRIT 31
BUMPER STICKER..32
CREATOR..33
FROM THE FREEWILL CHAMBER................................34

HIS MASTERPIECE..35
BEYOND REPAIR 36
DON'T KNOW WHAT TO DO..37
GOD'S LOVE..39
ACCORDING 40
LOVE WINS 41
DON'T DOUBT IT 42
A TURN 43
MISSISSIPPI..44
LIFE OR DEATH 45
EVERYTHING IS SACRED..46
THE GIFT OFFERED WITH TEARS 47
BECAUSE TONIGHT MORNING COMES 48
LOVE 49
ALWAYS WILL FROM GOD..50
IMMENSELY 51
FEAR IS THE ENEMY 52
A COMMAND 53
ALSO 54
MINIMALIST 55
FEAR..56
A PRAISE TO REMEMBER 57
IF YOU ARE FORTUNATE 60
JESUS LOVE 61
LIFE AFTER LIFE..62
LOVE IS A BATTLESHIP 63
MORTAL AND PASSING 64
MY BAND NAME 65
MY STORY..66
NOT AFRAID..67
PLAIN BROWN WRAPPER 69
POETRY THOUGHT 70
PROPAGANDISTS 71

PURSUE 72
QUIET 73
REUNION 74
Granpa Miller 75
SO GO AHEAD..76
SPEAK WHAT YOU WISH...78
SPEAKING OF TIME 79
STOLEN 80
SUBJUGATION 81
TERROR THEN JOY 82
THAT FREES..83
BOUNDARIES 84
THE GENTLE 85
THE LORD OF RIGHTEOUSNESS 86
THE LOVED ONES 87
THE MANY 88
THE PLACE 90
The Soul 91
THE TRUE...92
THOUGH DEATH AND ROT.......................................93
POSSUM VIEWS 94
THE STARE 95
TOLERATE..96
TRAIN A COMING 97
TTL...98
TWO 2 99
WHAT YOU'RE LOOKING FOR................................ 100
WINE AND BLOOD.. 101
WORDS... 102
WORTH... 103
YOUR CAT YOUR DOG... 104
ADDICTION IS A STINKING HOLE......................... 106
MADE FOR LOVE 108

LOVE QUINTILLION 109
BUMPER STICKER 110
YOUR SELF 112
BODY ENDS SPIRIT GOES 113
NOT IN PANIC 114
THE SADNESS 115
ADDICTION CRIPPLES ANOTHER ONE 116
BE THAT STRANGE FLOWER 117
I CARRY 118
THE MOST BEAUTIFUL 119
FLOCK TO THE SHORE 120
MASTER CLASS 121
FIND 122
APOCALYPTIC PHRASE | APRIL 2022 123
I WILL FORGIVE YOU 124
THE ANGEL SAID 125
LOVE HIM 126
TINY THINGS 127
COLD HARD STARE 128
CAN'T GO WRONG 130
WE WONDER 131
ENERGY 133
STONE COLD STARE 135
LOVE IS ALL 136
IF YOU FIND 137
BE WORTHY 139
DEATH BY EVIL 140
THE TEACHER 141
MOST CHERISHED THING 142
A BATTLE 143
THE WRETCHED 144
ALL ARE EQUAL 145
CREATED BY 146

HIGHEST GIFT 147
LOVE ALMIGHTY 148
MY BODY IS NOT ME 149
WISPY 151
YOU WILL 152
GLIMMER 153
USA 2020 UNTIL 154
NO TIME 156
THE HEART 157
BE COURAGEOUS 158
NO LIMIT 159
PRAYER 160
BE A BIRD THAT SINGS 161
NOT IN FIRE NOT IN WATER 162
NOTHING IS REAL 163
PILE OF MIRACLES 164
PERFECT 165
PANDEMIC 2020 166
ONLY WHAT 167
GREAT BLUE HERON 168
WORRY NOT 169
EVERY STICK 170
STILL LIVING 172
UNDERSTAND 173
USA POEM 174
NO SHAME 175
ONCE MORE 176
TO DO 177
I AM BLESSED 178
I ASK MYSELF 179
ALWAYS TRUST 180
IF YOU REVERE 181
WE MUST 182

UNDERSTANDING 183
BEST PATH 184
BLESSED BY LORD JESUS 185
HE CARES MORE 186
THANK YOU 187
AS IT SEEMS 188
I STRIVE 189
WHAT IT NEEDS 190
The Love 191
GOD FEELS 192
I DID NOT 193
IN THE BEGINNING 194

JESUS AND THOSE I LOVE

It is sadly beautiful
How you love me
How I love you
When I find you in the darkness
You hold me in the cold

I am terrified by the peace you are
I wander through the mystery
I dream no fear of anguish
As I press you to my soul

JESUS KNEW

He knew as fact
What we must accept on faith

That there is immense joy and satisfaction that awaits
Beyond the human body mind soul experience

This is no way diminishes the perfection of goodness and power
That he is
It begins to make clear
The truth
That if we trust in him
That he is what he says he is
His righteousness is ascribed to us

BUMPER STICKER

THE PRESENT IS SACRED
IMPERMANENCE IS SACRED

A PLACE I LOVE

The swale within the swale
reaches the beach

A place I love
Sheltered from all deceptions

Evil can be recognized
It is anything
That draws us from love

BIRTHDAY OF THE SONG

This is to celebrate
The birthday of the song
That has not been performed
That has not been written
It will break the spell

HAIL OF FORTY POUNDS

The boots of death are marching
The brave may see in time
The vile spirit of death approaching
The brave may stand to oppose it
Be slaughtered like the lamb

When violence is not abhorrent
There is danger at the door
When human sacrifice
Is acceptable
For the rancid cause

Scan the skies for the coal black clouds
They are pregnant with dread bolts
And
Hail of forty pounds

A MESSAGE FROM JESUS

The dirt is the same
As it was in the beginning

This crop may be threshed
And
Left to the birds

And
A new planting swiftly begun

JUST BECAUSE

God made you to be
Exactly who you are
The challenge is to determine
Who is the person of God's creation
Who is the misguided deceived one

What joy
When you meet your person of God's creation
Your strength, your fearlessness
Your acceptance of the real moment
Your inexpressible rest in the truth
That this is God's world, not yours

Somehow in some inexplicable way
You fit perfectly into God's project
Of leading humans into
Bliss
Just because

EARTH HUMAN LIFETIME

For humans
The natural progression is
To physical death
How much did the soul learn
From the Earth human lifetime?

JESUS IS

Jesus is Love and comfort
I am drawn to Him
Jesus is
God the Father's plan
To draw us to Him

The more we love Jesus
The more The Holy Spirit of God
May
Communicate with us
An incredible blessing

A TOAST FOR RED WINE

The blood of Jesus
That frees from darkness
All who believe
He is real and true

GOD'S LOVE

The boundaries
For me
Enclose the most beautiful places
God's love
Is
Spectacular

IRREPARABLE

Like the sun
Like the universe
Like heaven
Like truth

The blood of Christ
That frees from darkness
All
Who believe He is real and true

It is the strangest story
We have the option to believe

I believe it

COVID TIME

Covid time near the ocean waves
My ghost sits in the sand
A pantomime no one understands
Like an arrow shooting a bow

*

Pirates swarm my ship
Abuse my loved ones one by one
I lie helpless
I write this song in my mind

*

All is not lost
The writer is steadily writing
My blood is drained by parasites
My rage lives on

*

Make your case
Plead your virtue
I know you are death
You cannot fool me

*

We flounder
Neath the boot of fools
Cry out in shrill torment
Praying for their destruction

*

If ever they may
Pause to wonder
Yes yes yes
You are lost

I WONDER

I wonder
is bliss
more real
than
suffering

I know
they are
quite strangely
the same
and
opposite
at once

LOVE AND FRIENDSHIP

Love and friendship
Yes
I'll have another

The love of God
Is
The blessing
To be sought
Above all

LIFE

Words limit the message
It is living with disdain and life sacrifice
In confronting tyrants
And their hordes

For love of the new ones

The Creator is still the creator

We muddle in fear or faith

Muddle nonetheless

A TEAR

Sometimes a tear is more precious
Than a time of joy
Often a tear is more precious
Than a time of joy
Often a tear
Precedes joy
God's love is
An exciting
Precious
Balance
If we trust
We are blessed

DOMAIN

The world of thought
is the domain
There is great value
contributing there
We do it every day
Which domain
The kind or the violent
The free or the oppressed or the oppressor
The world of thought
is the domain
The forgiving or the revenging
The depressed or the growing
The living or the fearing

IF YOU LOVE

If you love Jesus
You love your life
You love the life
Of your loved ones
Life is
A courageous choice
And
I love them

WE LEARN

We learn through the hard times
We must try hard
To not
Unlearn through the good times

ELECTION 2020 USA

I have heard in my heart
This treachery will not stand

INAUGURATION DAY 2021

This is the day
A historic day
This is the inauguration day
Of
The
Most corrupt
Creepiest
Most degenerate
Most illegally elected
Candidate in American History

*

So many firsts
So many records

*

The first hair-sniffer
The most successful political criminal
The first viral video star
Surely you have seen it

*

It's titled
FIRE THE PROSECUTOR OR YOU DON'T GET THE BILLION
A LOVE LETTER TO UKRAINE

*

It also marks the day
The DOJ
The FBI
and
The Supreme Court
Officially suffocated themselves
In the putrid quicksand of the political swamp

*

My apologies to natural swamps

Natural swamps are glorious beautiful
and
Life Giving

24

FREEDOM

Subject to interpretation
is a truism
We are floundering
neath the boot of fools
We have a God given right
to live or die free
in freedom to speak
until the Earth is dead
I plan to live or die free

Don't quibble over what is free
I think we know

Surely we know
What
It is not

GOOD DOCTORS 2020

The good doctors
They are in a maddening predicament

They know the cures for the ravaging disease

The gatekeepers refuse it

The cures are too simple
and free
you see
Virtually free
and
Would free the humans
From the bondage of tyrants

GHASTLY TORMENT

Living in this age of deception and lies
Heartless ghastly indifference
To human suffering bondage and subjugation
Is a ghastly torment
If you are not among the deceived or the deceivers

The boundaries for me
Have fallen around beautiful places
I dare not fear the fiends
They relish devouring the fearful frail and feeble

If you are blessed
You know who they are
You sense the clawed grip of their evil hand approaching
your throat
Long before your suffocation is sanctioned and achieved

A MAN ON HIS HORSE

A man on his horse
With his gun
Has seen the guts in the dust
He rides on
Like the sun

GOD'S BEAUTIFUL VISION

God's beautiful vision
Is the beautiful beings
He created
Living in beautiful peacefulness
With one another
With beautiful tolerance and forgiveness
For one another
In perfect freedom faith and trust in him
Nonviolent and
Subjugated to him alone and
Fearing no other thing
But his opinion

BIG UNIVERSE BY CAT JUKI

My cat, Juki, stood on my lap and made biscuits.
She said to me, "The universe is big."
I said, "Cat, how do you know?"
She said, "The fact that the scenario exists, wherein, a small predator can make biscuits on the lap of the apex predator, and the apex predator supplies for the small predator, free food, shelter, and medical care, requires an enormous universe of possibilities."

HOLY SPIRIT

The Holy Spirit
Has always been here
Because all of the creation is of the Father
and
The Holy Spirit is the Spirit of the Father

If the Holy Spirit
Had been recognized by more humans
Then The Father
Would not have needed to place his being
Into a human
To walk the Earth
and
Suffer in faith

His most cherished piece of art
To offer a path
An offer of a path

BUMPER STICKER

THANK YOU JESUS
THAT'S MY PRAYER

CREATOR

Don't wait 'til death
To do your life review
Do it now
If there are things that trouble you
That don't mean shite
Make sure
They trouble you no more
As
They don't mean shite

Give the foolish choices you've made
To the supreme lover of the frail deceived
He is your truest friend
His love is for your eternal being
Powerful in love and forgiveness
As has been delegated to him
By the Father
The Creator
To be praised
As if
We have some infinitesimal
Understanding of
The magnificence
Of the Creator
Our charge
Is to love the creation
As does
The Creator
Thy will be done

FROM THE FREEWILL CHAMBER

We are in a freewill chamber
Freewill may not be defiled or defied
In this freewill chamber
We determine what
Comes next
Why is it so hard
Maybe it is not
When we submit freely
Our will
To the Creator
Thy will be done
I trust you
Only
You
Your plan for me
Is only good
Only love
No fear
Fear is the enemy
Love and trust is strength
No matter
The horrible challenge
Love trust strength dignity
In lack
In frustration
In pain
Jesus
I love you
I trust you
Unto natural human death
I long to merge
With your spirit
Thank you for
Your abandon
Your love
Your
Faith

HIS MASTERPIECE

Life is the exquisite art of God
And Jesus
Is
Of course
His masterpiece

BEYOND REPAIR

God's love
Is
Beyond repair
Walk on

DON'T KNOW WHAT TO DO

I don't know what to do
I don't know what to say
I don't know what to do
I don't know what to say

So I ask Jesus
He knows what to do
He knows what to say

So I ask Jesus
He knows what to do
He knows what to say
It just goes on this way
Don't know what to do
Don't know what to say

So I ask Jesus
He knows what to do
He knows what to say

He ee knows the way
He ee knows the way
He knows the way
Hey hey hey

You are on the life train
You are blessed

GOD'S LOVE

God's love
Is
The most important
Force
In the universe

ACCORDING

And God told me

Better that you not see

Though you nearly do

In this particular time

According
To My Plan

LOVE WINS

How important are fathers
They are vitally important
As are mothers sons and daughters

A loving father is a gift
From The Loving Father
As is
The loving mother
The loving daughter
The loving son

All are gifts to be cherished and remembered
And loved and highly valued
From the always
Loving Father

Love wins

DON'T DOUBT IT

Sending signals
Like a harbor marker

This is the way
Steer this way

I love you

Don't doubt it

A TURN

A turn
In the right direction
Is as precious
As the love
That lies deep in the heart
Of the person
You respect the most
Because
You know
Their motive
Is
Love
And they fear
Only
What must be feared

MISSISSIPPI

Land of the free and the brave
That's where I want to be

Will courage be required in Heaven
As it is on Earth
Faith will be required
As it is on Earth

If there is no suffering in Heaven
How will we grow further in strength, knowledge, wisdom

What is the upper limit of strength, knowledge, wisdom
Is it Jesus

It is an enormous blessing
To be of no offense to him

It's in the present
It's in the heart

LIFE OR DEATH

Every day
we choose
Life or Death

what we think
what we do

We are the only
beings of freewill
that we know of

The only beings
that in any moment
may choose
to end
our body's life

All our choices
are
Life or Death

EVERYTHING IS SACRED

Your joy
your bliss
your pain
your sorrow
All are sacred

*

Your energy
your fatigue
your spirit
your body
All are sacred

*

Your laughter
your tears
your fears
your cheers
All are sacred

*

Your first breath
your last breath
your vitality
your spiritless corpse
All are sacred

THE GIFT OFFERED WITH TEARS

Learn to forgive instinctively
Love every human as if
You are their parent
When they stumble
When they are deceived onto a path
That takes them farther and farther from the Light
Your heart does not condemn them
No
You weep for them
You cherish them
You pray for them

You have a tiny glimpse into
The sorrow of The Creator
You participate
in the hope of their salvation
You will share in the glorious joy of
Their rebirth
As the beings of light and love
They were created to be

Cry in anguish for their turning to the Light
Cry in joy
Because your Father hears you
He loves you
He is merciful
He longs more purely than my tears
That in their free will
They turn to him
They accept the gift offered

Saying in their heart
Father please help me
I choose the path
Of love faith humility light life

BECAUSE TONIGHT MORNING COMES

Are you courageous and strong
Are you timid and weak

Are you disfigured and slow of wit
Are you beautiful and brilliant

It matters so very lightly

Because tonight
The morning comes

On the glorious other side

LOVE

Love is always
What God
Is
Trying
To tell us

ALWAYS WILL FROM GOD

You know I love you
The way I love you
And I always will

You can rest in life and sorrow
And know I always will

Love you
The way I love you
And I always will

Never surrender to the darkness
Not in a trillion years

Because I love you
The way I love you

And

I always will

IMMENSELY

Jesus

Is immensely more powerful

Than the multitudes of
Scowling sinister violent hopeless
Human beings
and
The despicable horde of evil spirits
They have surrendered their will to

I trust Jesus

FEAR IS THE ENEMY

Fear is the enemy
The enemy is fear

Fear is the weapon of evil
Faith is the weapon of victors

How can this be

But I already know

A COMMAND

You may not fear

Fear is death

Except for the proper fear
The kind to preserve your life

As life is precious

If the thought
That life is sacred is lost

Horror and drudgery
Will be
Our lot

ALSO

Jesus
Is the kindest
Most benevolent
Being
You have met

Also

The most powerful

MINIMALIST

I want a minimal amount
Of fat
On my body
On my mind
On my soul

I want all my fears
Cast into a massive fiery volcano

I want to have absolute trust in The Creator of all
It only makes sense
It seems

There is no other way

FEAR

Do you believe this is
A transient state

Yes I believe
This is a transient state

Then you
May
No longer Fear

A PRAISE TO REMEMBER

Jesus Christ
Is
Lord and King
Lord and King
Lord and King
Lord and King of Everything

DEATHISM 2020

No one knows what to call it, so, I'll call it what I choose, Deathism. It is swarming like biting gnats. I am but one man to live, to die, to squirm in fear toward a noble death, a free man. I sit by my fire on my acre near the marshes and a short drive to the sandy beaches of north Florida. I drink. I heed the hordes of demons as they spread like a suffocating slime. Maybe I wish to die unknown, with no honor or acclaim; a pointless sacrifice, forgotten as the Earth continues on its course.

The Deathism sect is preparing for slaughter. They are demonizing a large portion of the population of the United States, preparing them for subjugation and/or slaughter. Among the Deathism goals is the dehumanizing, exclusion and demonizing of those which do not share the Deathist world view. They must convince their loyalists that the opposition are dangerous, violent, racists, bigots overwhelmed by superstition and backward notions.

Surely you see that the exclusion, the denial of God-given rights and the slaughter is already in process. The slaughter, disheartening and dehumanization are being carried out by means of the sickening, useless requirement of mask-wearing and the deadly implementation of, also useless, societal lockdowns. The fear of death should not be more intense than the fear of subjugation.

A COMMENTARY 2020 USA

I read the story of a man who lost six friends of his to suicide because of the trampling of the civil liberties of America. We have been muzzled, masked and silenced. Many have been forbidden the right to earn what is needed to feed their families. The powers that be are terrorizing our children. People have had to delay medical treatment and diagnostic testing. The harm being done to decent human beings on the pretense that this virus is an apocalyptic event is reprehensible. Life is never risk-free. Strong people live on faith, wits, common-sense and courage. God Bless and restore the ideals of faith, freedom, personal responsibility, and common decency, that this miraculous country was founded on.

IF YOU ARE FORTUNATE

If you are fortunate
There will be no tyrants
That you must kill
In your lifetime

If there are hordes of them
You are worthy of pity

But fear not
The Creator
Will ameliorate
Will destroy
In due time

One may be your charge
Hordes are not

Wait and trust
The Creator of all things

JESUS LOVE

Jesus love
Is the source of the energy
And
The action produced from the energy

LIFE AFTER LIFE

We may always
Call the state we are in
Life
But
It may always be true
That there is
Life after Life

LOVE IS A BATTLESHIP

Love is a battleship
Armed massive
Ploughing through the storm
Undaunted

MORTAL AND PASSING

We love the people
That are mortal and passing

That we may love them
As they are immortal

MY BAND NAME

She's a Thang

is

The name of my band

or maybe

Corned Beef Hash and The Crackers

or

Flowers in the Dark

or

The Petulance

or

The Pestilence

or

The Nebulous

or

Fat Cowboys and a Girl

or

The Ketones

or

Clouds of Virus

or

The Gnarltones

Yes!

THE GNARLTONES

MY STORY

I just realized
The second most important story

Is
My story

NOT AFRAID

Not afraid
To be
Not afraid
Til death
Do us part
Said my spirit
To my body

ONE TRILLIONTH

I was told, by a very reliable source, that the understanding of God's creation, of the most brilliant human being, as is, the collective knowledge and understanding of every human that has breathed this atmosphere or squinted at this sun, is, exactly, one trillionth of the reality of it, and as it is, God's creation is continuing to expand, so the amount that can be understood by humans remains exactly one trillionth of true comprehension.

Faith is required.

PLAIN BROWN WRAPPER

It is nearly all revealed
in the plain brown wrapper

Unwrap the now
The plain brown wrapper

The now
Here I Am
Everything is here
All the creation is now
Like a fountain

We are on a sphere
traveling through space

We don't comprehend
The sphere
or
The space

Nor infinity
Nor this moment

And yes
I'm fine
And I'll have another
With great gratitude

POETRY THOUGHT

Poetry thought
Courage action
Music sounds
Story
Health suffer
Go broke helping
Starve helping
Speak you must
The Lord
Jesus
Breath
Trust the sand
Movement
Strain constantly reasonably
Blessed forgiven
Loved life everlasting
Reunion
Blissful energy suffering
Heart mind
Thought language
Conscious movement
Conscious stillness
Building life abiding
Gratitude

PROPAGANDISTS

The propagandists are crushing us down
Every day every morning

The frost is on the prairie
The chances are all gone

What the hell
March on

PURSUE

Like the leopard
Like the cheetah
Pursue
With no fear of broken jaw
No fear of torn sinew
No fear of exhaustion
Pursue

QUIET

There is a quiet inside us
that longs
for the love world
we feel is true

REUNION

The universe
Is massive forces with
Infinitesimally delicate controls and balances

I am here to marvel within it
I do marvel in awe and gratitude

Another human on pilgrimage
Longing for reunion

Granpa Miller

The perfection of humanity was made clear as a fine diamond to me the twenty years I worked in garbage collection. Humans are perfect in love, perfect in evil, perfect in health, perfect in disease, perfect in brilliance of thought, perfect in hazy idiocy, blind rage, perfect in marching to the metronome of the battle drum to gore, slaughter, agony, and the glory of being spent in futility. I do know that they are perfect; we are as perfect as a wispy cloud or the fart of a raccoon in this pristine universe.

One day I said to my strong and precious wife Emily, "I was just remembering what my grandfather, who I love and miss greatly, said to me when we were fishing in his twelve foot flat bottom boat when I was maybe ten years old."

He said, "Creely my man; if you are fortunate, there will be no tyrants that you must kill in your lifetime."

My Granpa had only passed a few months before Emily and I met and four months later married. I mentioned to her that he had passed but I had no heart to speak about him because he was a part of my soul and my grieving was still fragile. But now, two years later, I finally felt I could speak of him and I am so very glad.

Emily said, "I wish I could have met Granpa Miller."

SO GO AHEAD

Since we don't

Know

Go ahead

And

Say something positive

Like

One day

These deceived

Will see

How confused

Duped

Used

Preyed upon

They were in this moment

And

All

Can be forgiven

In Jesus

SOMETHING I MISSED

Holy Spirit, I think I missed something you were telling me. I could not follow it or retain it because I had to concentrate too hard on driving as I was intoxicated. Please tell me again. I fear I have lost it forever. Please tell me again.

Many minutes passed. I sat in my chair safely at home.

These words came into my mind. Because you love me, because you cry out to me, I will have mercy on you, because you trust my love and mercy. You should not fear, because you know I am love and faithfulness. You understand love, forgiveness and faithfulness. Therefore, I will tell you what you should have missed because you were fully occupied with the concerns you had driving intoxicated. Because you love and trust me, I will tell you what you should have retained, and that is.

Because you believe me and trust me you should not fear. I know you believe and trust me, so do not fear. I love you. I love all my humans. To those that love and trust me I will reveal more and more of myself; which is love and mercy and honest holy judgement and compassion. I love you. Fear nothing. Only fear separation from me. I love you. Do not reject my love.

SPEAK WHAT YOU WISH

Like what you like
Learn what you learn
Speak what you wish
There should be no violent response

At least some and should all
Understand
That even if you are dreadfully uninformed
and
Wrong in your opinions and assessments

Theirs is not given to judge you
In any absolute terms

Only
I Am

SPEAKING OF TIME

The present
Is
Sacred

STOLEN

Stolen election
What do I care
God will direct the beguiled deceivers
To their training ground
To receive their due recompense

SUBJUGATION

Subjugation

Is not for me

I have no intention

Of surviving it

TERROR THEN JOY

Terror
Then
Joy
When
You
Find
That
You have
Long
Been
Wrong

THAT FREES

The blood of Christ
That frees
From deception and evil
All
Who believe
He is real and true

BOUNDARIES

The boundaries
For me
Have
Grown around
Beautiful things
God's love is the oldest
New
Spectacular thing

THE GENTLE

He will nearly clap
Much will be brought down
Much will be revealed
The gentle ones that die
Will be greatly blessed in eternity

THE LORD OF RIGHTEOUSNESS

The Lord our righteousness
Laid in hell for a time
In our stead
He
Above all others
Deserves our trust

THE LOVED ONES

All the loved ones
Loved because they are love

Being prepared to participate
In the blessing and blessings
Of the loved ones

I saw the loved ones
I felt their peace
During
"Love in - Love out"
Breath meditation

Dear Lord Jesus
Many are deceived
But
You know that

THE MANY

Many are comrades in peace
They cherish, they crave peace
Would die for or with their friend
Their spouse, their child, your spouse, your child
Your friend, your loved one

*

These are the humans that God and his angels may speak to
Imparting gifts of wisdom, patience, courage, acceptance,
compassion, hope, endurance, faith, knowledge, peace, forgiveness, love,
deliverance from evil

*

There are those that cherish and crave
comfort, riches, pleasure, and, reverence and fear from fellow humans

*

These will rob the blood-bought freedom of the many
If they are not whole-heartedly, courageously resisted
By the many

*

No surrender
No appeasement
No negotiation
No compromise
No treaty
They can never be trusted

*

The many who crave peace
and cherish the freedom to explore and grow
in this universe of mind, matter and spirit

*

Must prevail

Must resist subjugation
To the last breath

89

THE PLACE

God's love
Is anywhere
You can
Accept it

The Soul

If God had made only
One sun
And only
One planet
That circles that sun

Upon which
Sentient beings reside

That would surely
Be enough

Eternally

That is only
Only
The tip
Of the pen

THE TRUE

We all have an expiration date

We don't know what it is

So love

and

Show up

THOUGH DEATH AND ROT

Though death and rot
Be our body's lot

Still we endure
Still we love
Still we comfort and
Hold to faith and vision

Though death and rot
Be our lot
We sing of joy and glory
We hold fast
The hope of time and eternity
Because of the one who loves us

Though death and rot
Be our lot
Our souls
They smell
Of perfume
Of flowers
Though death and rot
Be our lot
Because of the one who loves us

POSSUM VIEWS

Possums do not understand
Human treachery
Their only thought of humans
Is that none can be trusted

Possums do not understand
The value of humans
This they share
With the treacherous

Possums accept
The struggle for sustenance
As do many humans
The treacherous do not

Possums have no opinion
As to whether some humans are expendable
And are worthy to be
Used and abused mercilessly

The treacherous have a very succinct
Entrenched
Agreed upon view
On this subject of deceit abuse and slaughter

THE STARE

Oh

How do I love you
Who stare unflinching
Into the cold red eyes
Of sycophants of demons

Calmly knowing
They will hiss and sting
Spew venom

Bare their rotting teeth
Spray the stench of rotting flesh

Because you dare to dare to intercede
To thwart their master's cause

God bless you all

TOLERATE

We the people are falling short
We should not tolerate
That which
We are ignoring

TRAIN A COMING

If you hear your train a coming
And
It's coming to take you to Jesus Kingdom
Or
Coming to take you to what The Father
designed you for on Earth
Then
You are fine

TTL

Terrorize the lemmings

For power
For personal gain

Adulation
and
Aggrandizement

You
Fiends

TWO 2

2 is the most important number
Because
2 squared = 4 and
4 squared = 16 and
16 squared = 256 and
256 squared = 65,536 and
65,536 squared = 4,294,967,296 and
4,294,967,296 squared = 1.84 x 10 to the 19th
or
1,840,000,000,000,000,000
which is
1 quintillion 840 quadrillion
Therefore if 2 loudmouths charismatically proclaim
Life love faith and courage
And
Two more are moved to
Zealous surrender and charismatic speech
Then
Perhaps
The Kingdom of God
Is upon us

WHAT YOU'RE LOOKING FOR

Did you find what you were looking for, or
Did what you're looking for find you

It doesn't matter
If what you're looking for is good

If what you're looking for is vile, rank violence
and fear

Then God help you

WINE AND BLOOD

I took a sip
and said

"The blood of Christ that frees from evil
all that believe
he is real and true"

WORDS

We think in words
As we live in words

Because

As we think

We live

WORTH

When is enough enough
in addiction to victimhood
in addiction to alcohol
in addiction to opiates, debilitating foods, lies
in addiction to cynicism to subjugation
in addiction to fear dread rigidity

It's all in the mind
addiction to what's good for you
addiction to strength positivity courage
addiction to faith in the creator
addiction to freedom
addiction to movement
addiction to flexibility
addiction to love kindness
addiction to abhorrence of violence
addiction to the sanctity of the individual human

YOUR CAT YOUR DOG

Your cat
Your dog
Cannot understand you
Nor
Can you understand
Your cat
Your dog
You cannot understand God
Yet
God can understand you

RAYLAN SAYS

I'm on a giant ball, a giant ball spinning and flying through the vastness of space.

Most of the Earth's societies were shut down by a microorganism that's about 120 billionths of a meter in diameter; that's 120 nanometers. By comparison we sentient beings are generally between 1.5 billion and 2.1 billion nanometers in length; therefore, proving that we are children of God with much to unlearn.

Still it is blissful sitting outdoors by this oak wood fire with the healthy young dog named Raylan.

Raylan tells me, "I think faith in the creator and love might be the deal."

I think a few minutes about what Raylan said.

He appeared to be expecting me to offer some comment on what he shared. He did that little wumpf wumpf bark they do when they're growing impatient.

Finally, while staring at the fire, I said, "Raylan, you might be on to something there, but, who's gonna listen? You're just a dawg!"

About a minute passed in silence, and we laughed and laughed, and I drank some more red wine and held my cup to the sky and said, "The blood of Jesus Christ that frees from darkness and deception all that believe he is real and true."

Raylan said, with conviction, "AMEN BROTHER!"

And we laughed.

After many seconds of silence Raylan said, "But I'm just a dawg!"

We laughed and laughed.

I took another righteous slug.

ADDICTION IS A STINKING HOLE

Addiction is a stinking hole
A deep dark stinking hole
Do you think you want to go there?

*

If you want to lose your soul
If you want to lose your mind
If you want to lose your sacred body
If you want to lose everyone you love
If you want to lose everyone who loves you

*

Then hell yeah
You go there
Hell yeah you go there

*

You will burn
You will scream in agony
So will those who love you
So hell yeah you go there

*

Feel all the pain your choice will cause
Spit on the ones that love you

*

You enter the hell you created
If you go down that burning stinking hole

*

Be sure to blow your writhing whimpering loved ones
A poison kiss As you descend

*

We love you

We miss you
Our suffering
Cannot save you

MADE FOR LOVE

My hands
My feet
Are made for love
But I am
Lost in the darkness
Lost in the darkness
I flail like a madman
I am lost in the darkness
I love
I Am
Love

LOVE QUINTILLION

Jesus can love
A quintillion quintillion souls
And
Never runs low

BUMPER STICKER

ADDICTION AND FEAR
ARE DEATH

ADDICTION WITH NO PROFANITY

My challenge is to write this using no profanity. This is a mighty challenge.

The stench of addiction is the stench of rotting mammals and rotting fish, and the stench of diseased bloody human diarrhea. The stench described here is one millionth the incense of addiction.

There is no adequate description of the feelings experienced watching a loved one transform into a vile, heartless, lying, stealing, manipulating, cold hearted, wretched subhuman.

The sense of failure alone, turns all colors gray, and joy and vigor to a constant, aching pain in the body and the soul. Suicide?

How can I describe addiction without cursing?

Only by believing and knowing that the Creator is more loving, merciful and tender than we can comprehend and existence is not only our bodies.

I have succeeded in describing addiction using no profanity.

I must be dead!

YOUR SELF

We all have our selfhood to endure
You may be a mother of seven in a rich home
or
A mother of eight in a poor home
You may be alone in an efficiency in New York
You may be old in pain
Remembering the loves of your life
The spouses The children The heartaches
Your self travels on
To the place you know not
But your self travels on
But not in vain
Your self is you
You are connected
Protected
Loved by God

BODY ENDS SPIRIT GOES

If you live to be old
Then you will know
That only God knows

When your body ends
Your spirit goes on forever

If you are young and you know this
You are blessed

NOT IN PANIC

Birds sense the coming bitter cold
This is why you see them at your feeders
Days before you feel the cold

I pray God allow the same for us
When brutal cold evil is
Flowing our way

That we may move toward
His Love
Not in a panic

THE SADNESS

The sadness is so deep
That my feet can't move
So deep
That my lungs can't breathe
So deep
That my heart stops beating
So deep
That my mind is fried
So deep
That I die
Without a whimper

ADDICTION CRIPPLES ANOTHER ONE

Addiction cripples another one
And satan shrieks with glee
The mothers and the fathers
The grandmothers and grandfathers
Writhe in agony
The wives the husbands
The daughters and sons
Writhe in agony
The addicted stands rotting

satan shrieks with glee

BE THAT STRANGE FLOWER

Be that strange flower
With bloom as black as coal
With stem and leaves
The colors only heaven knows
With roots that glow of brilliant energy
That warms the soil
That blesses the plants all around
Distribute your seeds
To bless the finch
The titmouse
The waxwing
The sparrow
Be that strange flower

I CARRY

God is in every cell of my body
Every atom
Every energy
Every vibration
And
All things are in my mind
The mind of Christ
I carry meaning

THE MOST BEAUTIFUL

Jesus is the most beautiful mountain
Jesus is the most beautiful ocean
Jesus is the most beautiful sky
Jesus is the most beautiful reason why

FLOCK TO THE SHORE

Flock to the shore
I want to know more
Of the way you love life
And don't care anymore

It's all about love you say
You don't fear death anyway
It's a journey for learning
Going home any day

I love you in this hour
I tremble in your power
I love you everywhere
I'll find you over there

Going home
Going home
I'm so happy
Going home

MASTER CLASS

Don't worry much over what you achieve
You are a miracle among the miracles
You are loved
You are blessed and cherished every moment
You are learning love
This is the Master Class

FIND

The love of God is like this

If you are burning hot
Seek the love of God
You will find coolness

If you are freezing in agony
Seek the love of God
You will find warmth

APOCALYPTIC PHRASE
APRIL 2022

I love apocalyptic stories lately
They seem so germane

I WILL FORGIVE YOU

You can hang me
You can burn me
You can scourge me
You can nail me to a cross

I will proclaim
The love of freedom
The love of the Father
I will
Forgive you

THE ANGEL SAID

You are set to die for
Love life kindness and utility

Are you strong enough and able

I said
If God says so

The angel said

You are set to die for
Love life kindness and utility

LOVE HIM

Jesus is good
Beyond our cognition
Love Him

You will be blessed

TINY THINGS

It's the tiny things
That matter most

The big things are naught

The tiny are your charge

They hold all the blessing

COLD HARD STARE

They are trying to destroy the free
But I stand here an ancient oak tree
I stand here with my cold hard stare

I will live in this prison quietly
I will not squirm when you kill me
I will haunt you with my cold hard stare

They are weak They are deceit They are deceived
They destroy and kill But they will lose

He will have mercy still

They will learn love in searing pain and distress
under
His cold hard stare

I SOMETIMES WONDER

I sometimes wonder what those who love me who have passed to where many more things are understood are thinking of me

Is it, 'I hope he will understand soon, before he must learn through God's merciful suffering?'

Or do they think, 'Praise God, he has seen and he will move ahead without fear because he knows that love is life, life is love.'

CAN'T GO WRONG

Pursue these things
and
You can't go wrong
Peace patience kindness courage faith
Goodness tolerance compassion
Forgiveness generosity
Humility
Love always
Wonder
Stubbornness to continue
Joy
Jesus

WE WONDER

We wonder why we are here
I think mainly
We are here to marvel

I AM
I am love
I am light
I love
I am

ENERGY

We don't see energy
We see or feel
An effect of the energy
Through energy
We cannot see

THE PERFECT RETORT TO EVIL

You can go anywhere
Go to hell I don't care
Feel my cold hard stare

As you descend

I fight for right
With no weapons
But my cold hard stare
And a word

STONE COLD STARE

I have no energy for histrionics
I must only stand square
with a stone cold stare

Look into my eyes as you kill me

These eyes will be etched in your mind
In your soul
Until you are no more
Or
Repent

LOVE IS ALL

I Am Love
The Lord of all
The I Am
Love is all

IF YOU FIND

If you find your way

In the Kingdom of God
While a human on Earth

You are mightily blessed

GREAT DAY

It has been a great day of suffering

And

The Love of God

BE WORTHY

Be worthy
To have a friend true

DEATH BY EVIL

The last free human
That dies confronting evil
Is a treasure
As is the first

We will hear heaven's music
We will drink heaven's wine
We will laugh and dance together
In Heaven's light

THE TEACHER

You fight evil
With love and more love

At least
When they kill your human body
They will feel shame and remorse for a microsecond

What a long hard journey
They are requiring themselves

They will ponder with no understanding
Until they do understand

Until they understand
God is Love
Is the teacher

MOST CHERISHED THING

What is the most cherished thing
Depends on your circumstance

If you are being freed to death
It is light

As it always is

A BATTLE

Seeking the reality of spirituality
Is a battle
Of two men
Equally strong
The closer we get to pure love
The closer we are to home

THE WRETCHED

Your mind and your love
Are your powers

Do not let the wretched
Stop you or alter you

Allow them control over neither

ALL ARE EQUAL

We all humans can love
This is how we all are equal
It is the power that transforms

CREATED BY

I am learning love
and
The absence of love
My time here on Earth

In this body

Created by I AM

HIGHEST GIFT

The Love of God
Amplified to you
Is the highest gift

LOVE ALMIGHTY

Poultice and powders and leaf and grape and grain
To make this phase more bearable

Should we drop them all
Feel the anguish joy frustration and pain
Straight on and
Perish more swiftly and efficiently

Or
Just carry on as long as allotted
Dull the pain

Seek always in all ways

Trust the vision of Love Almighty

MY BODY IS NOT ME

Just as
My body is not me
But is what you and I
Can perceive

The universe is not God
But is what you and I
Can perceive

As God is Love
Which we cannot perceive

IS ALL

I am
Love is all

WISPY

The love of God
Is an image in our
Wispy passing minds

Seek that image

YOU WILL

Place a hand over your heart
A hand over your solar plexus

No matter what suffering
You have endured
Say

Thank you Creator of all things
I trust you
I love you

You will be blessed

GLIMMER

I see a glimmer
Of the beauty
Of the Creator my God
In every star
In everything created

USA 2020 UNTIL

They are trying to trigger the free
To compliance or insanity

They abuse children mothers fathers sisters brothers friends
They are barbaric heinous hideous repulsive wretched disgusting

Maggots writhe within their hearts
Snakes defecate within their souls
Rats urinate within their bowels
Demons sweat poison within their brains

Our will is what they fear most

We must retain
Our
Stone Cold Hard Stare

I AM

I am
My body and the Earth and the sky
And the spirits all around

My guides and those that love me
And those I am blessed to know and love

That is my world
That is my life
That is my future
That is my God

His name is Love
His name is I AM

NO TIME

There is no time like the present
This is really true
No other time
Comes close
In magnitude
or
Prescience

There is no time like the present

THE HEART

I stared at the heart of brokenness
It was a bright and shining radiant star

BE COURAGEOUS

Be courageous
or
Be fearful
It matters little
but
Be courageous

NO LIMIT

There is no limit
To God's love and mercy
To those
That cry out to him

PRAYER

Dear Father
I pray that your kindness and wisdom
be on this situation

That your love and comfort would be manifest
to those whose hearts seem broken
and
Bless with faith
Those in fear

Somehow
I know
There is no end

Thank you Jesus

BE A BIRD THAT SINGS

161

NOT IN FIRE NOT IN WATER

I cannot cleanse myself
Not in fire
Not in water

*

This Earth is not Heaven
This Earth is not damnation

*

It is
Heaven and damnation at once

*

The darkness of the evil tormenting the kind
Is here

*

The blessing of the light of love
Is here

*

I cannot cleanse myself
Not in fire
Not in water

*

I can be here
I fall at your feet

NOTHING IS REAL

Nothing is real but
It all hurts

Joy and laughter are real
They do not hurt

But
Nothing is real
But
It all hurts

PILE OF MIRACLES

I am not a pile of junk
I am a pile of miracles

PERFECT

The Love of God
Is so perfect
Understatement
Is unavoidable

PANDEMIC 2020

How do I know
In the midst of all the lying and manipulation
That God loves each human absolutely

I know I just know
There is no doubt

Those that abuse human beings
By decision or power

Physical or manipulative

Will pay their penalty
In
Horrendous
Strange
Ways

ONLY WHAT

I am not a galaxy
I am not a star
I am not the universe
I am far beyond

I am a human
On the Earth

I want my fellow humans
To suffer

Only

What they must

GREAT BLUE HERON

What does the Great Blue Heron think
When the belly is full
When the urge to mate has waned
Perhaps to dream to be a spritely Tern

WORRY NOT

I am in a dimension a condition
I know I am transient here

The body you see
Will change to rot

There are many other dimensions conditions

I know God willed me here
I worry not

EVERY STICK

Thank you God
For every stick
I place on my fire
I know
Every stick is from you

ONLY THIS

It always comes to and from
The Love of God

Always the source
Always the solution

I trust this only

STILL LIVING

I am still a living being on Earth
Acting as if
I know what that means

UNDERSTAND

It's not so important
That you are loved

It is important
That you love
That you seek to understand it

You will find your joy and peace there
You will find the Creator
Desirous of your pleasant conversation

USA POEM

I trust you Creator
Though I melt or burn away
I know I know

Though

NO SHAME

I am not ashamed
I am not embarrassed
Of being an Earth Human

However

I do continually

Strive

To raise my station

ONCE MORE

The poet sits by the river

He drowns in the river

He goes home

Tomorrow he returns to the river

He sits once more

TO DO

You don't have to do
Everything that you think
but
You have to think
Everything that you do

I AM BLESSED

God wants me
To capture His messages

I Am blessed
In this

I ASK MYSELF

Is God happy
Is God joyous

I surmised
God is happy
When one human realizes
How much He loves him or her

And when that human knows this
They become a blessing to all humans

And this blesses all humans
Because He made all humans in His likeness
With a glimmer of His power
His Love
His joy in loving kindness and joy
For all His loved ones
Of which
You are one

ALWAYS TRUST

I am a human being
On Earth
In God's creation
Because
God wills it

I am glad
As The Creator
Can
Always
Be trusted

IF YOU REVERE

If you seek
If you revere
God's Love
You yourself
Will become loving
You will be so much closer
To the peace and bliss
That you
Have always sought

WE MUST

We must live our daily lives
As if
We are unafraid
As if
We understand
Enraptured in God's creation

UNDERSTANDING

I understand
Fear is not from you Lord Jesus
But
Discretion is

Fear is from
The force which deserves no name

I pray for Your protection
From the unnamed

For all I know and Love
And all I do not know
And all I would require
Your grace vision
To Love

BEST PATH

The best path for humans
Is what God has ordained

Love kindness compassion Love
Forgiveness mercy
Faith in His vision
In His desire

We are all frail and limited
He knows this

Strive nonetheless
It will not go unnoticed

BLESSED BY LORD JESUS

Those I pray for to Jesus
Are blessed

Because I know Him
I Love Him
He loves me
He loves them

He blesses those that trust Him

That is His nature
Ordained by The Father
The Creator of all
Amen
So be it
So it is

HE CARES MORE

Jesus has proven
He cares more for humans than any
I trust Him
I Love Him

THANK YOU

Thank You Lord Jesus
You are the only hope
The only rescue

I trust You
I trust You
I trust You

You cleanse
The past
The present
The future

You are all in all
Blessed are those
Who trust You

AS IT SEEMS

Everything is as what it seems
But it is
Not
What it means

I STRIVE

I strive to be free and able
To express God's Love and vision

Free in spite of fear
Able as I am enabled

Fear shall have no dominion

WHAT IT NEEDS

Give your body what it needs
It will give you what you need

Give it more than it needs
It will give you less than you need

Give it less than it needs
It will give you less than you need

Give it nothing it needs
I will see you at the next station

The Love

Love
The Love

The Love of
The understanding of Love

Is

The highest calling

I Am

GOD FEELS

Since God loves every human
More perfectly
Than the most loving human parent

Does God feel pain
When his children are hurting themselves

I don't know how this can be

But it seems so

I DID NOT

I did not create myself

*

I did not create my two parents

*

I did not create my four grandparents

*

I did not create my eight great grandparents

*

Nor my 16 great great grandparents

*

I did not create myself

*

But

*

I do love

IN THE BEGINNING

There was no thing
in the beginning

No thing to see feel hear or read
Now there is this book
Written by a human
That was not in the beginning

WOW